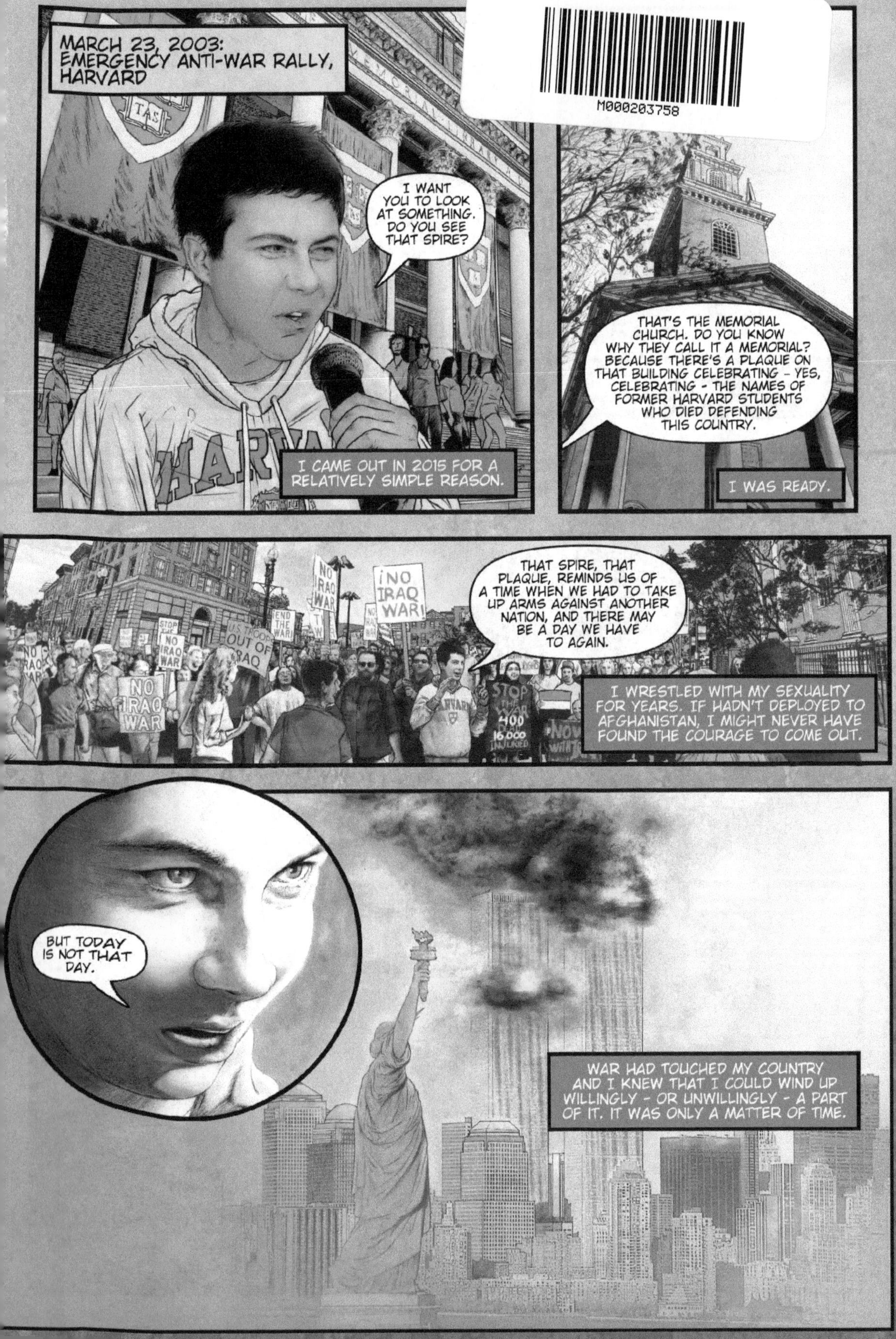
MARCH 23, 2003:
EMERGENCY ANTI-WAR RALLY, HARVARD
I WANT YOU TO LOOK AT SOMETHING. DO YOU SEE THAT SPIRE?
I CAME OUT IN 2015 FOR A RELATIVELY SIMPLE REASON.
THAT'S THE MEMORIAL CHURCH. DO YOU KNOW WHY THEY CALL IT A MEMORIAL? BECAUSE THERE'S A PLAQUE ON THAT BUILDING CELEBRATING - YES, CELEBRATING - THE NAMES OF FORMER HARVARD STUDENTS WHO DIED DEFENDING THIS COUNTRY.
I WAS READY.
THAT SPIRE, THAT PLAQUE, REMINDS US OF A TIME WHEN WE HAD TO TAKE UP ARMS AGAINST ANOTHER NATION, AND THERE MAY BE A DAY WE HAVE TO AGAIN.
I WRESTLED WITH MY SEXUALITY FOR YEARS. IF HADN'T DEPLOYED TO AFGHANISTAN, I MIGHT NEVER HAVE FOUND THE COURAGE TO COME OUT.
NO IRAQ WAR
¡NO IRAQ WAR!
END THE WAR!
OUT OF IRAQ
BUT TODAY IS NOT THAT DAY.
WAR HAD TOUCHED MY COUNTRY AND I KNEW THAT I COULD WIND UP WILLINGLY - OR UNWILLINGLY - A PART OF IT. IT WAS ONLY A MATTER OF TIME.

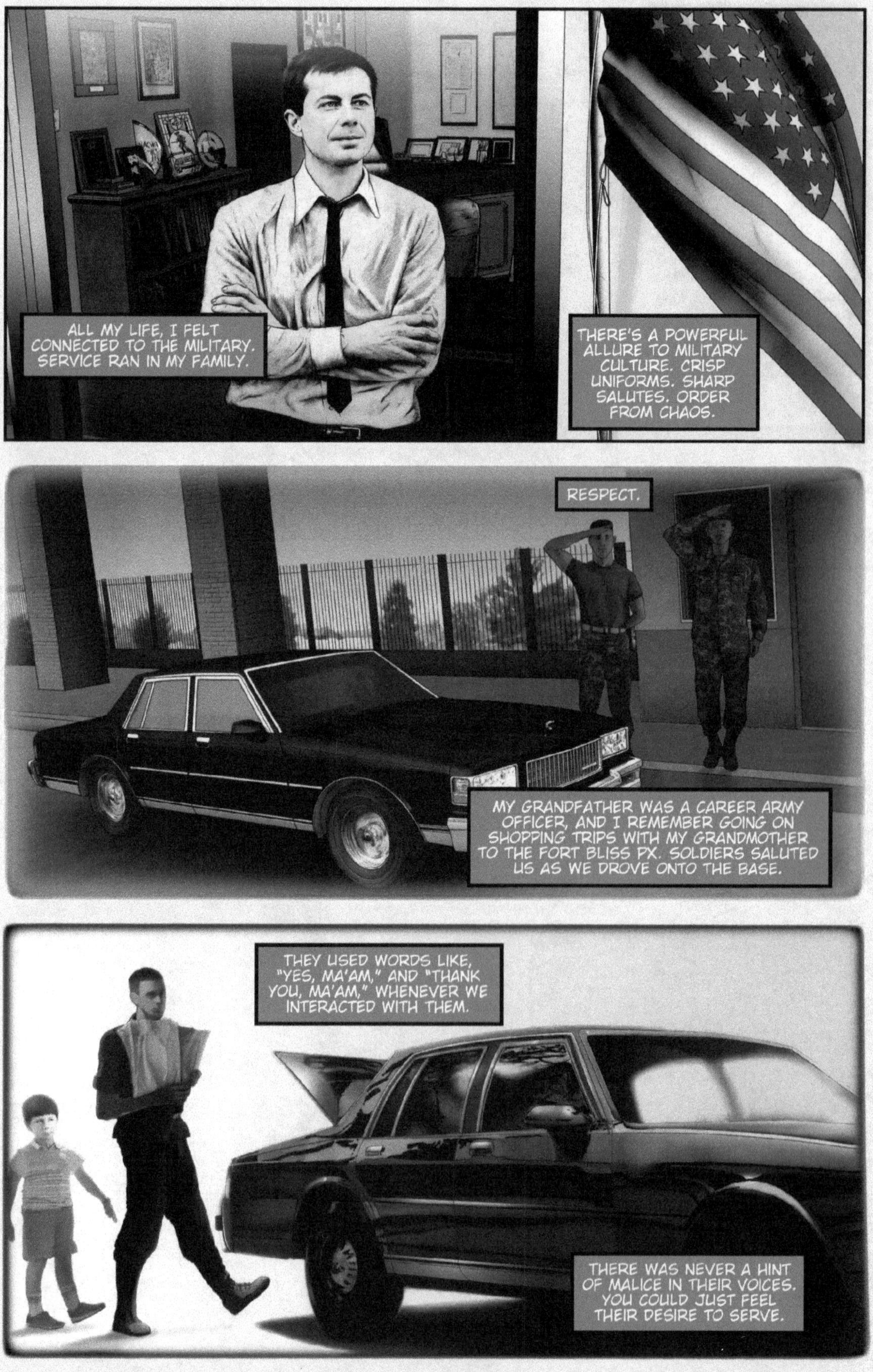
ALL MY LIFE, I FELT CONNECTED TO THE MILITARY. SERVICE RAN IN MY FAMILY.
THERE'S A POWERFUL ALLURE TO MILITARY CULTURE. CRISP UNIFORMS. SHARP SALUTES. ORDER FROM CHAOS.
RESPECT.
MY GRANDFATHER WAS A CAREER ARMY OFFICER, AND I REMEMBER GOING ON SHOPPING TRIPS WITH MY GRANDMOTHER TO THE FORT BLISS PX. SOLDIERS SALUTED US AS WE DROVE ONTO THE BASE.
THEY USED WORDS LIKE, "YES, MA'AM," AND "THANK YOU, MA'AM," WHENEVER WE INTERACTED WITH THEM.
THERE WAS NEVER A HINT OF MALICE IN THEIR VOICES. YOU COULD JUST FEEL THEIR DESIRE TO SERVE.

AN OIL PAINTING OF MY GREAT UNCLE, RUSSELL MONTGOMERY, HANGS IN MY MOTHER'S LIVING ROOM. HE WAS AN ARMY AIR CORPS CAPTAIN DURING WORLD WAR II.

THE ARTIST USED COLORS AND EMPLOYED A STYLE THAT EVOKES THE WORK OF NORMAN ROCKWELL. HIS EYES, FOREVER UNBLINKING, SHOW BOTH STRENGTH AND KINDNESS. HE'S AS RELAXED AS A DEVOTED MILITARY MAN CAN BE ON DUTY, HIS HAND RESTING GENTLY ON HIS HAT. IT'S A MOMENT OF REPOSE CAPTURED FOREVER IN TIME.

WE HAD HIS LOGBOOK. I WOULD SPEND HOURS READING OF HIS EXPLOITS IN THE AIR DESPITE ONLY UNDERSTANDING SOME OF THE MILITARY JARGON FROM THE CONTEXT PROVIDED.

I ROMANTICIZED THE IDEA OF BECOMING A PILOT, DEFENDING MY COUNTRY FROM ENEMIES BOTH FOREIGN AND DOMESTIC.

UNCLE RUSSELL DIED IN A CRASH IN 1941, A HAZARD TOO COMMON FOR AIRMEN. I NEVER GOT A CHANCE TO MEET HIM. BUT HE LIVES ON IN OUR LIVING ROOM AND IN THE IMAGINATION OF A YOUNG BOY WHO FELT A CALLING TO SERVE.

BUT WHAT'S THAT OLD SAYING?

"LIFE IS WHAT HAPPENS WHEN YOU'RE MAKING OTHER PLANS."

I WAS BORN ON JANUARY 19, 1982, IN SOUTH BEND, INDIANA. MY PARENTS, JOSEPH BUTTIGIEG AND JENNIFER ANN MONTGOMERY, ARE BOTH INTELLECTUALS WHO TAUGHT AT NOTRE DAME.

MY FATHER EMIGRATED FROM MALTA, A SMALL ISLAND COUNTRY IN THE MEDITERRANEAN LOCATED JUST SOUTH OF SICILY.

AFTER GRADUATING FROM HEYTHROP COLLEGE IN OXFORD, ENGLAND, HE MOVED TO THE U.S. FOR HIS POST-DOC DEGREE AT THE STATE UNIVERSITY OF NEW YORK AT BINGHAMTON.

HE WAS A PROFESSOR OF ENGLISH AND ALSO SERVED AS THE CHAIR OF THE DEPARTMENT. HE RETIRED AFTER 40 YEARS OF TEACHING.

DAD WAS ALSO KNOWN FOR HIS WORK AS A TRANSLATOR AND PUBLISHED THREE VOLUMES WRITTEN BY ANTONIO GRAMSCI, AN ITALIAN PHILOSOPHER AND KNOWN COMMUNIST AND MARXIST.

THAT'S WHY THOSE ON THE RIGHT LOVE TO CALL ME A MARXIST, AS IF ASSOCIATION SOMEHOW EQUALS THE TRUTH. WONDER HOW THAT'S WORKING FOR THEM IN A TRUMP-DOMINATED PARTY? BUT I DIGRESS.

AFTER AN ILLNESS, MY FATHER PASSED ON JANUARY 27, 2019. HIS LAST WORDS?

"IT'S BEEN A GOOD TRIP."

Joseph Anthony Buttig[

Age: 71 - South Bend, India

All who knev
him as a brill
man, pasiona
cation, publi
its forms, an
His wife, Ar
son, Pete Bt
law, Chaste
all of South
as a loving
who was fo
travel, frien
was a geni
enthusiasti
friend, hus
and son.
Kaniewsk
South Ber
arrangeme
be held F
4 to 7 p.n
the camp
Notre Da
will be p
pring. I
nay be i
Commu
online c
www.Ki

May 20, 1947 - January 27, 201

e relished the c
olleagues and st
took great pleasu
sequent achievements of the

MY MOTHER IS A BORN AND BRED HOOSIER. HER FATHER WAS A COLONEL IN THE ARMY, SO SHE TRAVELED A LOT.

SHE ATTENDED COLLEGE AT THE UNIVERSITY OF TEXAS - AUSTIN AND MET MY FATHER WHEN THEY BOTH TAUGHT AT NEW MEXICO STATE UNIVERSITY.

MY PARENTS MARRIED IN 1980 AND MOVED TO SOUTH BEND TO TEACH.

HER WORK SPARKED MY INTEREST IN COMMUNICATION AND LANGUAGES. SHE STRENGTHENED MY ENGLISH SKILLS AND HELPED ME LEARN TO CONVERSE IN SEVEN OTHER LANGUAGES INCLUDING MALTESE, WHICH PLEASED MY FATHER'S SIDE OF THE FAMILY.

MY MOTHER WAS MY BIGGEST SUPPORTER IN MY RUN FOR THE PRESIDENCY.

AS I MOVED INTO HIGH SCHOOL AT ST. JOSEPH'S, THE INFLUENCE OF MY SCHOLAR PARENTS MADE IT A FOREGONE CONCLUSION THAT I'D FOLLOW IN THEIR FOOTSTEPS INSTEAD OF PURSUING A LIFE IN THE MILITARY.

I TURNED TO BOOKS, EXPLORING CLASSIC LITERATURE (THANKS, DAD) AND HISTORY.

IF YOU KNOW ANYTHING ABOUT EITHER SUBJECT, YOU KNOW THAT POLITICS INFLUENCE THE TRAJECTORY OF OUR HISTORY, THE ARTS, AND HUMAN THOUGHT. IN RETROSPECT, PERHAPS I SHOULD'VE SEEN MY CAREER COMING.

INSPIRED BY POLITICAL THOUGHT, I WROTE AN ESSAY IN 2000 FOR THE KENNEDY FAMILY'S "PROFILE IN COURAGE" SERIES THAT GARNERED AN HONOR FROM THE JFK LIBRARY. THE TOPIC?

"BERNIE SANDERS."

I EXPLORED HIS CANDOR AND INDEPENDENCE THAT SAW HIM WIN IN HIS HOME STATE EVEN AS HE PROUDLY DECLARED HIMSELF A SOCIALIST.

I WROTE, IN PART:

I commend Bernie Sanders for giving me an answer to those who say American young people see politics as a cesspool of corruption, beyond redemption. I have heard that no sensible young person today would want to give his or her life to public service.

I can personally assure you this is untrue.

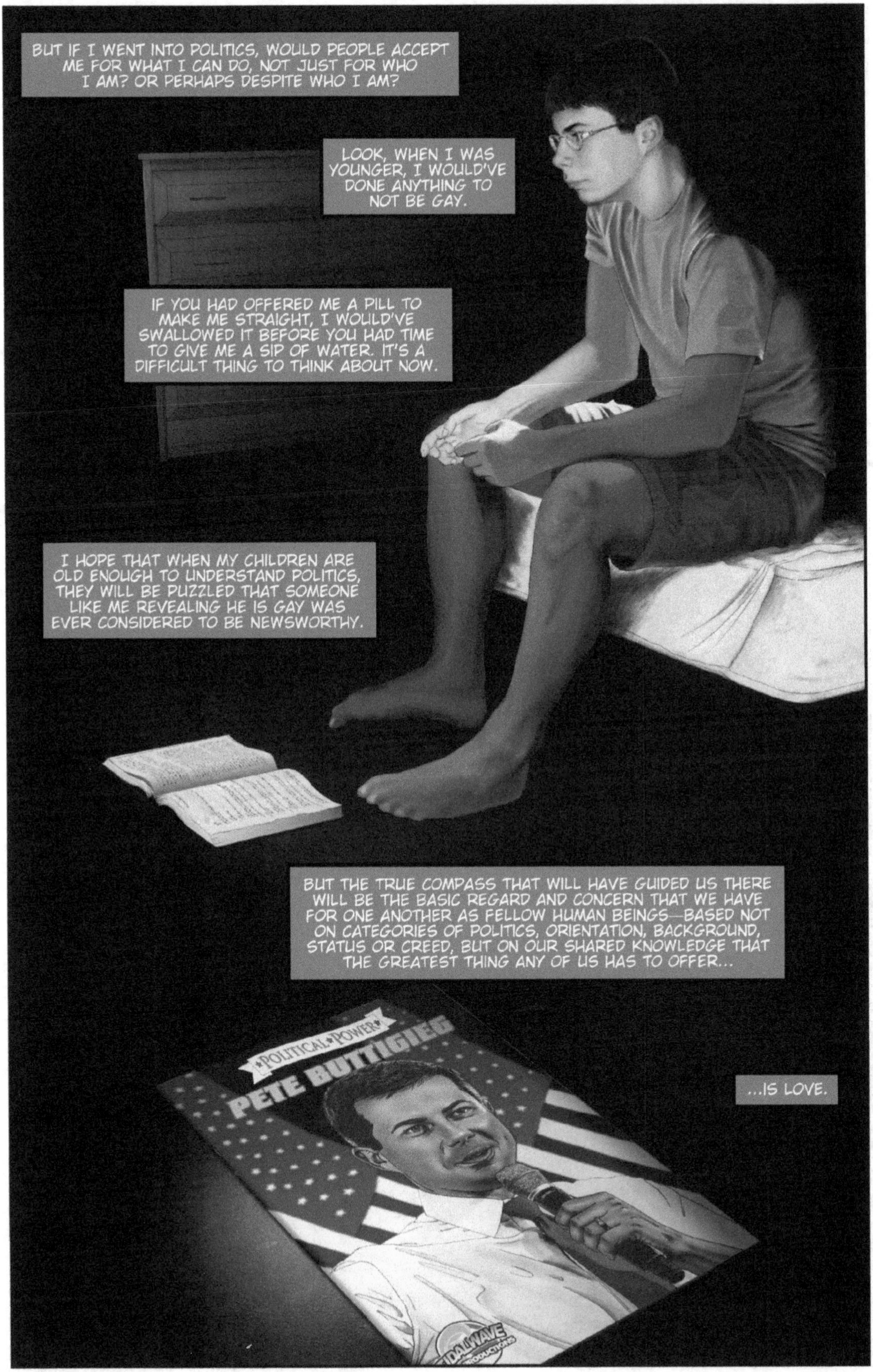
BUT IF I WENT INTO POLITICS, WOULD PEOPLE ACCEPT ME FOR WHAT I CAN DO, NOT JUST FOR WHO I AM? OR PERHAPS DESPITE WHO I AM?
LOOK, WHEN I WAS YOUNGER, I WOULD'VE DONE ANYTHING TO NOT BE GAY.
IF YOU HAD OFFERED ME A PILL TO MAKE ME STRAIGHT, I WOULD'VE SWALLOWED IT BEFORE YOU HAD TIME TO GIVE ME A SIP OF WATER. IT'S A DIFFICULT THING TO THINK ABOUT NOW.
I HOPE THAT WHEN MY CHILDREN ARE OLD ENOUGH TO UNDERSTAND POLITICS, THEY WILL BE PUZZLED THAT SOMEONE LIKE ME REVEALING HE IS GAY WAS EVER CONSIDERED TO BE NEWSWORTHY.
BUT THE TRUE COMPASS THAT WILL HAVE GUIDED US THERE WILL BE THE BASIC REGARD AND CONCERN THAT WE HAVE FOR ONE ANOTHER AS FELLOW HUMAN BEINGS—BASED NOT ON CATEGORIES OF POLITICS, ORIENTATION, BACKGROUND, STATUS OR CREED, BUT ON OUR SHARED KNOWLEDGE THAT THE GREATEST THING ANY OF US HAS TO OFFER...
POLITICAL POWER
PETE BUTTIGIEG
TIDALWAVE PRODUCTIONS
...IS LOVE.

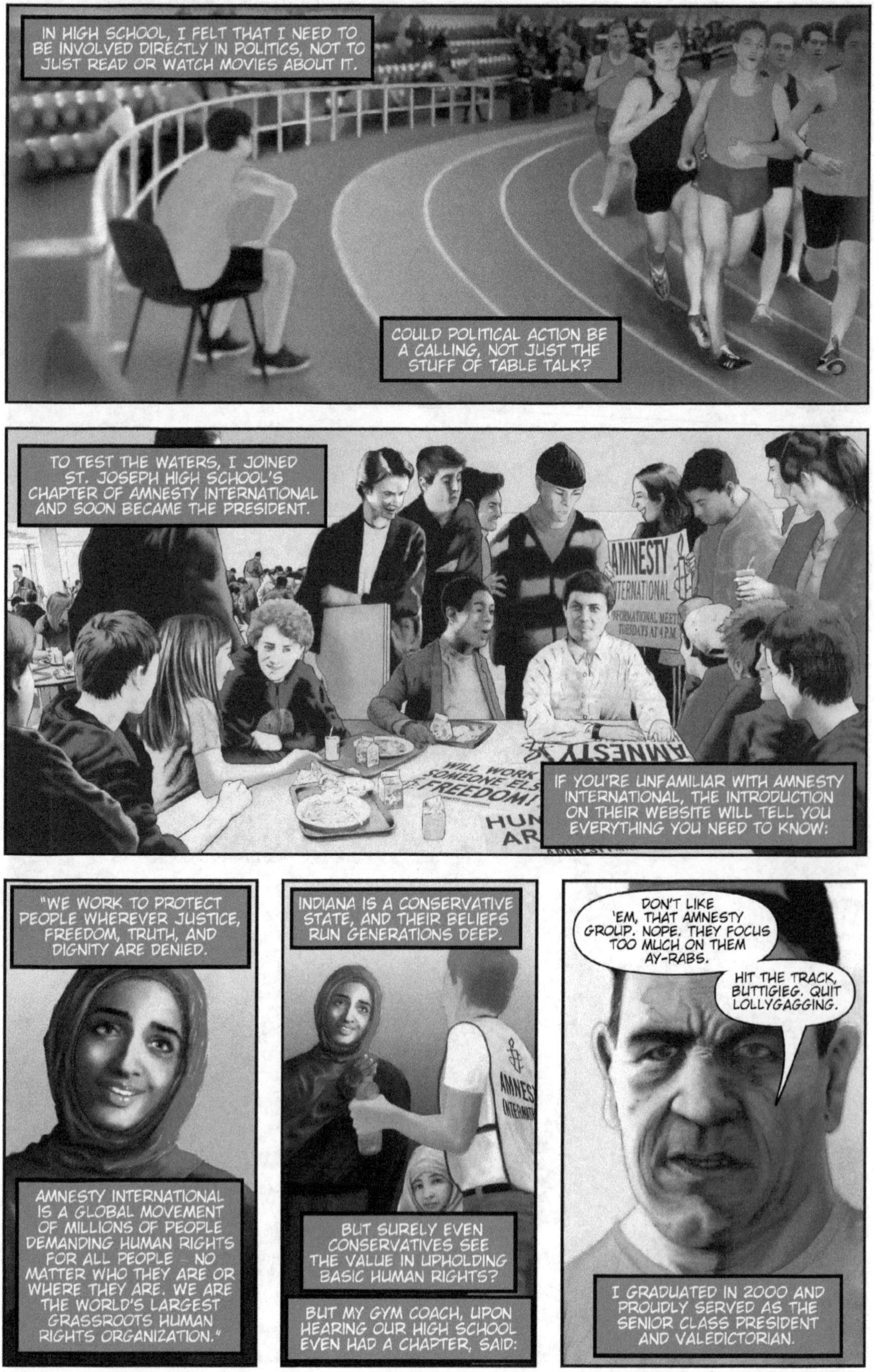
IN HIGH SCHOOL, I FELT THAT I NEED TO BE INVOLVED DIRECTLY IN POLITICS, NOT TO JUST READ OR WATCH MOVIES ABOUT IT.
COULD POLITICAL ACTION BE A CALLING, NOT JUST THE STUFF OF TABLE TALK?
TO TEST THE WATERS, I JOINED ST. JOSEPH HIGH SCHOOL'S CHAPTER OF AMNESTY INTERNATIONAL AND SOON BECAME THE PRESIDENT.
AMNESTY INTERNATIONAL
IF YOU'RE UNFAMILIAR WITH AMNESTY INTERNATIONAL, THE INTRODUCTION ON THEIR WEBSITE WILL TELL YOU EVERYTHING YOU NEED TO KNOW:
"WE WORK TO PROTECT PEOPLE WHEREVER JUSTICE, FREEDOM, TRUTH, AND DIGNITY ARE DENIED.
AMNESTY INTERNATIONAL IS A GLOBAL MOVEMENT OF MILLIONS OF PEOPLE DEMANDING HUMAN RIGHTS FOR ALL PEOPLE – NO MATTER WHO THEY ARE OR WHERE THEY ARE. WE ARE THE WORLD'S LARGEST GRASSROOTS HUMAN RIGHTS ORGANIZATION."
INDIANA IS A CONSERVATIVE STATE, AND THEIR BELIEFS RUN GENERATIONS DEEP.
BUT SURELY EVEN CONSERVATIVES SEE THE VALUE IN UPHOLDING BASIC HUMAN RIGHTS?
BUT MY GYM COACH, UPON HEARING OUR HIGH SCHOOL EVEN HAD A CHAPTER, SAID:
DON'T LIKE 'EM, THAT AMNESTY GROUP. NOPE. THEY FOCUS TOO MUCH ON THEM AY-RABS.
HIT THE TRACK, BUTTIGIEG. QUIT LOLLYGAGGING.
I GRADUATED IN 2000 AND PROUDLY SERVED AS THE SENIOR CLASS PRESIDENT AND VALEDICTORIAN.

HARVARD UNIVERSITY

LIKE MOST FRESHMEN, I WAS EXCITED TO START COLLEGE BECAUSE IT OFFERS AN OPTIMISTIC PROMISE OF CHANGE. YOU GET OUT OF IT WHAT YOU PUT INTO IT.

OF COURSE, WHEN YOU ATTEND AN IVY LEAGUE SCHOOL, YOU'RE AFFORDED NO SMALL AMOUNT OF PRIVILEGE. I WAS DETERMINED TO DISCOVER MY PASSION AND FIND MY PLACE.

MY DORM WAS THE SAME ROOM USED BY ULYSSES GRANT, JR., HORATIO ALGER, AND CORNEL WEST.

YOU COULD ALMOST FEEL THE WEIGHT OF HISTORY AND GREATNESS WHEN YOU WALKED ACROSS HARVARD SQUARE. THE CAMPUS IS TRULY A MARKETPLACE OF IDEAS, HOPES, AND DREAMS.

SOON, HARVARD STARTED TO FEEL LIKE PROFESSOR XAVIER'S SCHOOL IN THE X-MEN. EVERYONE HAD A POWER THAT MADE THEM DIFFERENT. SPECIAL. REMARKABLE.

CATE, WHO LIVED ON THE SECOND FLOOR OF THE DORM, COULD READ A BOOK FOUR OR FIVE TIMES FASTER THAN ANYONE ELSE. SHE REMEMBERED THEM, TOO, WITH ASTONISHING ACCURACY.

ANDREW, WHO LIVED ON THE BOTTOM FLOOR, COULD DEFEAT A RUBIK'S CUBE...

...IN LESS THAN A MINUTE! LET'S DO THAT AGAIN.

IT WAS A LITTLE THING, BUT IT WAS AMAZING TO WATCH.

MY ROOMMATE, STEVE, WAS LIKE PROFESSOR X HIMSELF – A TELEPATH. HE OBSERVED SOCIAL INTERACTIONS AND COULD PREDICT WITH UNCANNY ACCURACY HOW RELATIONSHIPS BETWEEN STUDENTS IN THE FRESHMEN CLASS WOULD PLAY OUT.

...AND HE'LL CHEAT ON HER WITH THAT GIRL IN CHEM LAB HE'S ALWAYS CHATTING UP.

AND ME? PERHAPS MY SUPERPOWER WAS, AS MYERS-BRIGGS MIGHT CLASSIFY IT, AS "THE COMMANDER."

I WAS STRONG-WILLED, IMAGINATIVE, FOUND A WAY TO SOLVE PROBLEMS, AND DETERMINED TO CARRY THE LEGACY OF THOSE WHO ONCE LIVED IN MY DORM ROOM.

I WAS DRIVEN BY MY DESIRE TO SERVE. ASSUMING THE ROLE OF STUDENT PRESIDENT AT HARVARD'S SCHOOL OF POLITICS, I WAS PROVIDED A POLITICAL EDUCATION NECESSARY TO MY FUTURE GOAL – A GOAL I COULDN'T ARTICULATE AT THE TIME. HEADED BY RETIRED SENATOR DAVID PRYOR, I'M TOLD THAT THE POSITION WAS SOUGHT ONLY BY THE MOST AMBITIOUS OF STUDENTS.

I WAS ALSO A COLUMNIST FOR THE CAMPUS NEWSPAPER, THE HARVARD CRIMSON, WHERE I WROTE ABOUT POLITICS. ONE POEM, ABOUT GEORGE W. BUSH, STANDS OUT. IT READS, IN PART:

You thought I was a moderate
You took it line and sinker
You never figured me for this
Reactionary thinker.
"Reformer with results,"
I said, and you all took the bait:
"Compassionate Conservative"
I cried at each debate.
Well think again, since now you know
The shade of my true colors;
(October 2003)

WE WERE YOUNG AND IDEALISTIC AND WANTED OUR GOVERNMENT TO BE TRUTHFUL IN THE WAKE OF 9/11. WE DEMANDED ACCOUNTABILITY FOR OUR WAR-FOOTING. MEN AND WOMEN WERE DYING, AND THE POLICIES AT THE TIME WERE MUDDIED BY DOUBT.

DO YOU SEE THAT SPIRE?

A RHODES SCHOLARSHIP SENT ME TO OXFORD, WHERE I STUDIED ECONOMICS.

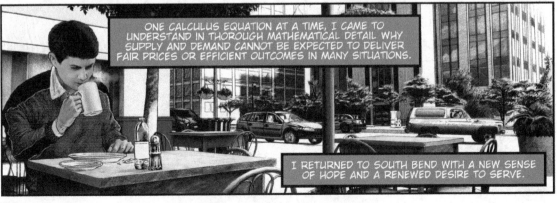

ONE CALCULUS EQUATION AT A TIME, I CAME TO UNDERSTAND IN THOROUGH MATHEMATICAL DETAIL WHY SUPPLY AND DEMAND CANNOT BE EXPECTED TO DELIVER FAIR PRICES OR EFFICIENT OUTCOMES IN MANY SITUATIONS.

I RETURNED TO SOUTH BEND WITH A NEW SENSE OF HOPE AND A RENEWED DESIRE TO SERVE.

INSTEAD, I STARTED WORKING FOR McKINSEY & COMPANY AS A MANAGEMENT CONSULTANT. THE PAY WAS GOOD...

...BUT THE JOB WAS, ULTIMATELY, NOT SATISFYING THIS GNAWING NEED IN MY GUTS.

NO ONE WAS PLEADING WITH A TWENTY-SEVEN-YEAR-OLD MANAGEMENT CONSULTANT TO RUN FOR STATEWIDE OFFICE AS A DEMOCRAT. I JUST STARTED TO THINK ABOUT IT AND FELT LIKE IT COULD MAKE SENSE.

I DECIDED TO RUN FOR THE INDIANA STATE TREASURER POSITION. IT PAID LESS THAN HALF OF WHAT McKINSEY & COMPANY PAID.

2010 WAS A TUMULTUOUS YEAR IN THE UNITED STATES. THE ECONOMY TANKED, HITTING THE AUTO INDUSTRY HARD. A BAILOUT WAS NECESSARY. THE FED PUT UP $80.7 BILLION TO HELP.

GRIPPED BY IDEOLOGY, MR. MOURDOCK JUST CAN'T ACCEPT THAT GOVERNMENT INVOLVEMENT IS A GOOD THING FOR THE PEOPLE IMPACTED BY THE DOWNTURN, EVEN IF THE BAILOUT IS PREVENTING THE DESTRUCTION OF THOUSANDS OF LIVES!

MY OPPONENT IN THE RACE FOR STATE TREASURER, INCUMBENT RICHARD MOURDOCK, FILED A LAWSUIT CHALLENGING THE BAILOUT'S LEGALITY. I USED THAT AS A LINCHPIN FOR MY ATTACK.

MOURDOCK WON 62.5% TO MY 36.5%.

THE INHABITANTS OF SOUTH BEND, INDIANA AND THE SURROUNDING COUNTRY WERE FORWARD IN THEIR THINKING AND AN ANOMALY IN THIS DEEP RED STATE. AFTER MY DEFEAT – WHICH TAUGHT ME A LOT ABOUT INDIANA POLITICS – I WONDERED WHAT WAS NEXT FOR ME.

THE PRIVATE SECTOR HELD NO ALLURE FOR ME. I FELT WOEFULLY INADEQUATE IN AN OFFICE SETTING. WHILE AT MCKINSEY & COMPANY, I STRUGGLED TO MAKE MEANING FROM MY EXPERIENCE THERE.

AT LEAST I KNEW WHAT I DIDN'T WANT TO DO. THAT'S SOMETHING.

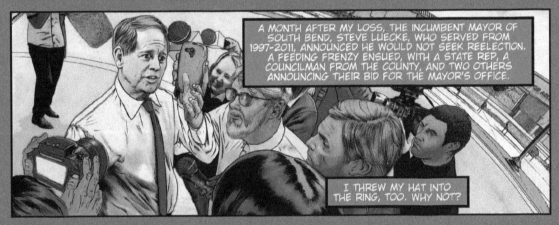

A MONTH AFTER MY LOSS, THE INCUMBENT MAYOR OF SOUTH BEND, STEVE LUECKE, WHO SERVED FROM 1997-2011, ANNOUNCED HE WOULD NOT SEEK REELECTION. A FEEDING FRENZY ENSUED, WITH A STATE REP, A COUNCILMAN FROM THE COUNTY, AND TWO OTHERS ANNOUNCING THEIR BID FOR THE MAYOR'S OFFICE.

I THREW MY HAT INTO THE RING, TOO. WHY NOT?

AN UNPRONOUNCEABLE, ETHNICALLY AMBIGUOUS NAME LIKE MINE IS AN ASSET IN NORTHERN INDIANA POLITICS.

BOOTY-GEEG? BUDDY-GUY-EGG? UH... PETER B.? HELLO?

BY THE WAY... IT'S PRONOUNCED "BUDDHA-JUDGE," OR IF YOU PREFER, "BOOT-A-JUDGE." MOST PEOPLE SAY IT LIKE "BOOT-EDGE-EDGE," AND THAT'S FINE, TOO.

DEPENDING UPON THEIR OWN BACKGROUND, PEOPLE COULD ASSUME MY SURNAME WAS HUNGARIAN, POLISH, SERBIAN, CZECH, OR EVEN BELGIAN. ALL CARRIED THEIR OWN COMMUNITY LOYALTIES IN THE REGION.

I WON THE MAJORITY OF THE VOTES IN THE 5-WAY RACE TO BECOME – AT THE TIME – THE YOUNGEST MAYOR IN THE COUNTRY.

SOUTH BEND, INDIANA: 2010

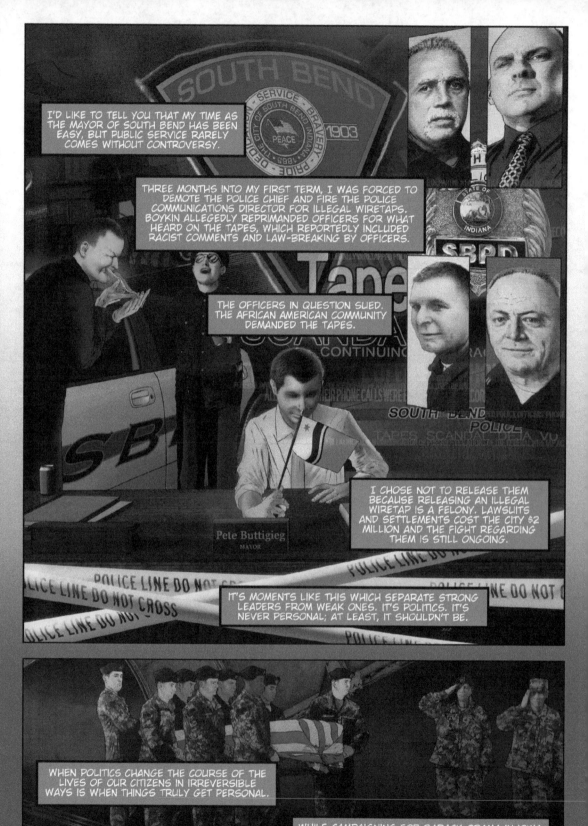

I'D LIKE TO TELL YOU THAT MY TIME AS THE MAYOR OF SOUTH BEND HAS BEEN EASY, BUT PUBLIC SERVICE RARELY COMES WITHOUT CONTROVERSY.

THREE MONTHS INTO MY FIRST TERM, I WAS FORCED TO DEMOTE THE POLICE CHIEF AND FIRE THE POLICE COMMUNICATIONS DIRECTOR FOR ILLEGAL WIRETAPS. BOYKIN ALLEGEDLY REPRIMANDED OFFICERS FOR WHAT HEARD ON THE TAPES, WHICH REPORTEDLY INCLUDED RACIST COMMENTS AND LAW-BREAKING BY OFFICERS.

THE OFFICERS IN QUESTION SUED. THE AFRICAN AMERICAN COMMUNITY DEMANDED THE TAPES.

I CHOSE NOT TO RELEASE THEM BECAUSE RELEASING AN ILLEGAL WIRETAP IS A FELONY. LAWSUITS AND SETTLEMENTS COST THE CITY $2 MILLION AND THE FIGHT REGARDING THEM IS STILL ONGOING.

IT'S MOMENTS LIKE THIS WHICH SEPARATE STRONG LEADERS FROM WEAK ONES. IT'S POLITICS. IT'S NEVER PERSONAL; AT LEAST, IT SHOULDN'T BE.

WHEN POLITICS CHANGE THE COURSE OF THE LIVES OF OUR CITIZENS IN IRREVERSIBLE WAYS IS WHEN THINGS TRULY GET PERSONAL.

WHILE CAMPAIGNING FOR BARACK OBAMA IN IOWA, I SAW FIRSTHAND HOW RURAL COMMUNITIES WERE LOSING THEIR YOUNG PEOPLE TO A WAR I'D PROTESTED A FEW YEARS EARLIER.

Pete Buttigieg
MAYOR

I MIGHT HAVE DRAGGED MY FEET FOREVER IF NOT FOR THAT EXPERIENCE.

IN 2009, THE YEAR PRIOR TO WINNING THE MAYORAL RACE, I ENLISTED IN THE U.S. NAVY RESERVE AND ENTERED A TRAINING PROGRAM TO BECOME A NAVAL INTELLIGENCE OFFICER. I WANTED TO BE ON THE RIGHT SIDE OF HISTORY.

I PRESSED MY SUPERIORS TO SEND ME OVERSEAS SOONER THAN LATER. I WAS ORDERED TO DEPLOY IN LATE-MARCH OF 2014 AND SERVED IN THE AFGHANISTAN THREAT FINANCE CELL IN KABUL.

BEFORE I SHIPPED OUT, I WAS SENT TO A CAMP OUTSIDE FORT JACKSON AND TRAINED TO BECOME A "DIRT SAILOR," A COLORFUL EPITHET FOR "NAVY PERSONNEL ASSIGNED TO ARMY-STYLE JOBS IN COMBAT ZONES."

THAT MEANS I WAS SENT TO WHAT THEY CALL AN "IMMINENT DANGER PAY AREA."

THE ROLE OF THOSE SERVING IN THE ATFC IS TO IDENTIFY AND DISRUPT THE TALIBAN, AL-QAEDA, AND OTHER INSURGENT GROUPS FINANCIAL SUPPORT NETWORKS.

IT'S NOT LIKE I KILLED BIN LADEN, SO DON'T PICTURE MY TIME THERE LIKE THAT.

BEHIND THE WIRE, I SAT IN A SECURE AREA AT A SOPHISTICATED COMPUTER TERMINAL.

IT WAS STILL DANGEROUS. THOSE DEPLOYED LEARNED WHAT IT IS TO TRUST ONE ANOTHER WITH OUR LIVES.

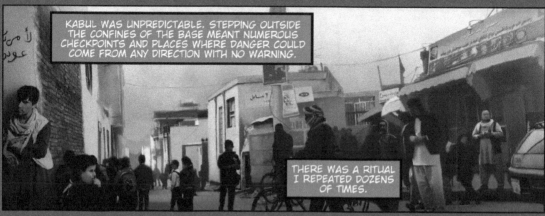

KABUL WAS UNPREDICTABLE. STEPPING OUTSIDE THE CONFINES OF THE BASE MEANT NUMEROUS CHECKPOINTS AND PLACES WHERE DANGER COULD COME FROM ANY DIRECTION WITH NO WARNING.

THERE WAS A RITUAL I REPEATED DOZENS OF TIMES.

I WOULD HOIST MY ARMORED BODY INTO THE DRIVER'S SEAT OF OUR MILITARY TAN LAND CRUISER, CHAMBER A LIVE ROUND IN MY M4, AND LOCK THE DOORS. WHEN WE CROSSED OUTSIDE THE RELATIVE SAFETY OF THE WIRE INTO A HOSTILE AFGHAN CITY, I ENTERED A WORLD MORE EXCITING AND THRILLING – AND MOST ASSUREDLY MORE DANGEROUS – THAN THE ZONE BEHIND THE BLAST WALLS.

WE LEARNED TO KEEP AN EYE ON NERVOUS LONE DRIVERS ON THE ROAD.

WE SCANNED FOR ROUGH, MALE HANDS SUDDENLY APPEARING FROM UNDER A WOMAN'S BURQA.

WE PRACTICED OUR MARKSMANSHIP SKILLS IN HOPES WE NEVER HAD TO PULL A WEAPON, BUT IF WE DID, THAT WE KNEW HOW TO USE IT.

I WANT TO MAKE SOMETHING CLEAR TO YOU. THE WAR IN AFGHANISTAN WASN'T A MISTAKE. BUT AS I TOOK STOCK OF MY PLACE AND TIMING IN A WAR THAT HAD CLAIMED SO MANY BRAVE YOUNG MEN AND WOMEN, I REALIZED THAT MOST PEOPLE STATESIDE BELIEVED THE WAR WAS ENDING. IT NO LONGER DOMINATED OUR NEWS CYCLE.

SO I HAVE TO WONDER: HOW CAN WE ASK A PERSON TO BE THE LAST TO DIE FOR ANYTHING?

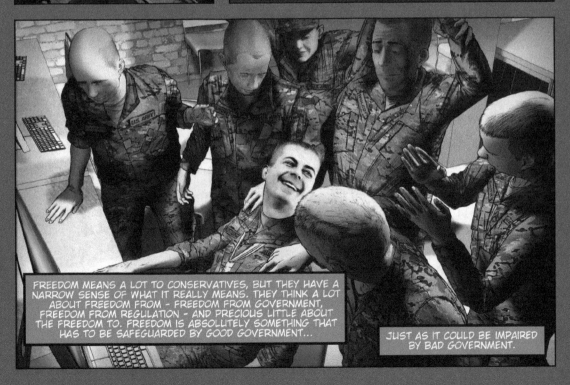

FREEDOM MEANS A LOT TO CONSERVATIVES, BUT THEY HAVE A NARROW SENSE OF WHAT IT REALLY MEANS. THEY THINK A LOT ABOUT FREEDOM FROM – FREEDOM FROM GOVERNMENT, FREEDOM FROM REGULATION – AND PRECIOUS LITTLE ABOUT THE FREEDOM TO. FREEDOM IS ABSOLUTELY SOMETHING THAT HAS TO BE SAFEGUARDED BY GOOD GOVERNMENT...

JUST AS IT COULD BE IMPAIRED BY BAD GOVERNMENT.

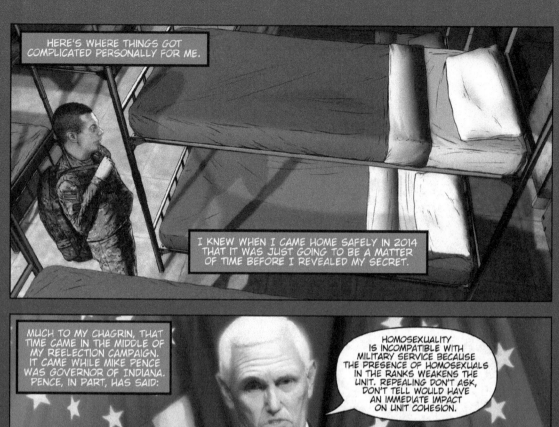

HERE'S WHERE THINGS GOT COMPLICATED PERSONALLY FOR ME.

I KNEW WHEN I CAME HOME SAFELY IN 2014 THAT IT WAS JUST GOING TO BE A MATTER OF TIME BEFORE I REVEALED MY SECRET.

MUCH TO MY CHAGRIN, THAT TIME CAME IN THE MIDDLE OF MY REELECTION CAMPAIGN. IT CAME WHILE MIKE PENCE WAS GOVERNOR OF INDIANA. PENCE, IN PART, HAS SAID:

HOMOSEXUALITY IS INCOMPATIBLE WITH MILITARY SERVICE BECAUSE THE PRESENCE OF HOMOSEXUALS IN THE RANKS WEAKENS THE UNIT. REPEALING DON'T ASK, DON'T TELL WOULD HAVE AN IMMEDIATE IMPACT ON UNIT COHESION.

BEING GAY ISN'T SOMETHING YOU CHOOSE, BUT YOU DO FACE CHOICES ABOUT WHETHER AND HOW TO DISCUSS IT.

CONSERVATIVES IN INDIANA AND ELSEWHERE SEE THE RELIGIOUS FREEDOM RESTORATION ACT AS A VEHICLE FOR FIGHTING BACK AGAINST THE LEGALIZATION OF SAME-SEX MARRIAGE!

REVEALING MY SECRET CAME AT A TIME WHEN STATES LIKE ALABAMA WERE ROLLING BACK SAME-SEX MARRIAGE AND KANSAS AND ARKANSAS WERE MOVING TO BLOCK ANTI-DISCRIMINATION LAWS AIMED AT PROTECTING THE LGBTQ COMMUNITY.

THERE HAS NEVER BEEN AN ELECTED OUT EXECUTIVE IN OUR STATE. NO ONE WAS SURE WHAT EFFECT MY REVELATION WOULD HAVE ON MY FUTURE.

WOULD PEOPLE IN OUR SOCIALLY CONSERVATIVE COMMUNITY EMBRACE ME? WOULD THEY CONTINUE TO JUDGE ME BASED ON THE JOB I DID FOR THEM?

OR WOULD THEY TURN ON ME, UNABLE TO LOOK PAST THE FACT THAT WHO I WAS SOMETHING THEY HAD BEEN BROUGHT UP TO REJECT?

THERE WAS ONLY ONE WAY TO FIND OUT FOR SURE.

I WROTE AN OP-ED FOR THE NEWSPAPER AND WAITED TO SEE WHAT WOULD HAPPEN.

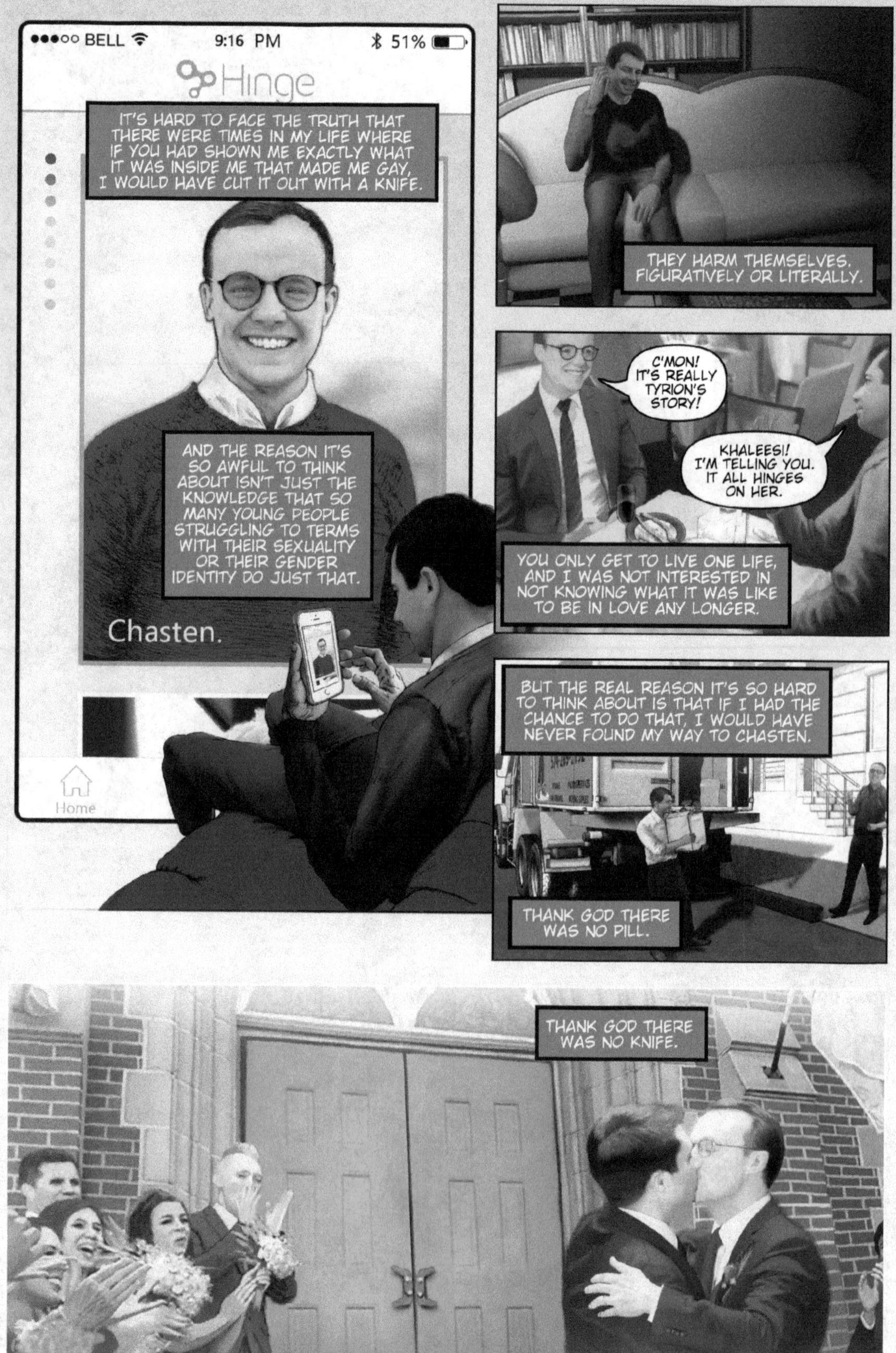
●●●○○ BELL 9:16 PM 51%
Hinge
IT'S HARD TO FACE THE TRUTH THAT THERE WERE TIMES IN MY LIFE WHERE IF YOU HAD SHOWN ME EXACTLY WHAT IT WAS INSIDE ME THAT MADE ME GAY, I WOULD HAVE CUT IT OUT WITH A KNIFE.
AND THE REASON IT'S SO AWFUL TO THINK ABOUT ISN'T JUST THE KNOWLEDGE THAT SO MANY YOUNG PEOPLE STRUGGLING TO TERMS WITH THEIR SEXUALITY OR THEIR GENDER IDENTITY DO JUST THAT.
Chasten.
Home
THEY HARM THEMSELVES. FIGURATIVELY OR LITERALLY.
C'MON! IT'S REALLY TYRION'S STORY!
KHALEESI! I'M TELLING YOU. IT ALL HINGES ON HER.
YOU ONLY GET TO LIVE ONE LIFE, AND I WAS NOT INTERESTED IN NOT KNOWING WHAT IT WAS LIKE TO BE IN LOVE ANY LONGER.
BUT THE REAL REASON IT'S SO HARD TO THINK ABOUT IS THAT IF I HAD THE CHANCE TO DO THAT, I WOULD HAVE NEVER FOUND MY WAY TO CHASTEN.
THANK GOD THERE WAS NO PILL.
THANK GOD THERE WAS NO KNIFE.

WEST SIDE DEMOCRATIC CLUB: 2015

ON REELECTION NIGHT, WE GOT 80% OF THE VOTE.

I DIDN'T THINK IT WOULD BE POSSIBLE TO WIN WITH THIS KIND OF MARGIN AND I THINK IT SHOWS THAT THE COMMUNITY IS REALLY UNITED. IT DOESN'T MEAN WE AGREE ON EVERYTHING BUT THE COMMUNITY AGREES OVERALL ON THE DIRECTION WE'RE HEADING AS A CITY.

FOUR YEARS AGO, I TURNED UP AS A POLITICAL UNKNOWN, A ROOKIE PROPOSING A FRESH START.

AND WHEN I SHOWED UP ASKING FOR THAT FRESH START, YOU GAVE ME AN OPPORTUNITY TO, YOU ENDORSED ME AS A LEADER AND YOU SUPPORTED ME AS A FRIEND. A YEAR AGO WHEN IT CAME TIME FOR ME TO STEP AWAY FROM THE JOB AND THE HOME THAT I LOVE TO GO OVERSEAS AND TAKE UP ARMS UNDER THE COLORS OF OUR NATION YOU SUPPORTED ME AS A BROTHER.

EARLIER THIS YEAR WHEN I WAS AT THE MOST VULNERABLE MOMENT IN MY PUBLIC AND PRIVATE LIFE, YOU EMBRACED ME AS A SON.

WELCOME TO

SOUTH BEND

Building a 21st Century City

Mayor Pete Buttigieg

"THE CITY OF SOUTH BEND MEANS THE WORLD TO ME, I LOVE SOUTH BEND."

I CAN TELL YOU THAT IF ME BEING GAY WAS A CHOICE, IT WAS A CHOICE THAT WAS MADE FAR, FAR ABOVE MY PAY GRADE.

AND THAT'S THE THING THE MIKE PENCES OF THE WORLD WOULD UNDERSTAND. THAT IF YOU'VE GOT A PROBLEM WITH WHO I AM, YOUR PROBLEM IS NOT WITH ME.

YOUR QUARREL IS NOT WITH ME. YOUR QUARREL, SIR, IS WITH MY CREATOR.

VICTORY
FUND
MAKE
HISTORIC FIRSTS
HISTORY

EPILOGUE

ACCORDING TO O'NEILL, HE ORDERED LOGAN TO DROP A KNIFE AS LOGAN APPROACHED HIM. HE DIDN'T, AND O'NEILL FIRED, STRIKING LOGAN IN THE ABDOMEN.

ON JUNE 16, 2019, SARGEANT RYAN O'NEILL ENCOUNTERED ERIC LOGAN IN THE PARKING LOT OF THE CENTRAL HIGH APARTMENTS AFTER O'NEILL RESPONDED TO A CALL ABOUT SOMEONE BREAKING INTO CARS.

SARGEANT O'NEILL'S BODY CAMERA WOULD HAVE BEEN ACTIVATED HAD O'NEILL USED LIGHTS AND SIRENS.

HE DIDN'T.

MR. LOGAN DIED AT THE SCENE.

WHILE THE MEN AND WOMEN VYING FOR THE DEMOCRATIC NOMINATION ENJOYED A FISH FRY IN SOUTH CAROLINA, I TRIED TO EXPLAIN TO THE CROWD AT A TOWN HALL MEETING THAT OFFICERS IN SOUTH BEND ARE REQUIRED TO HAVE THEIR BODY CAMERAS ACTIVATED WHEN RESPONDING TO A CALL.

WE DON'T TRUST YOU.

JUNE 23, 2019: SOUTH BEND, INDIANA

WHY HAVEN'T YOU BEEN ENFORCING IT, THEN?

I AM LISTENING. I WORK FOR YOU.

AS MAYOR OF THIS CITY, I WANT TO ACKNOWLEDGE THOSE LAST TWO LINES OF EFFORT – EFFORTS TO RECRUIT MORE MINORITY OFFICERS TO THE POLICE DEPARTMENT AND EFFORTS TO INTRODUCE BODY CAMERAS – HAVE NOT SUCCEEDED.

I GUESS I CAN'T BLAME THEM. THERE'S A LOT BENEATH THE SURFACE WHEN IT COMES TO TRUST AND LEGITIMACY AROUND POLICING AND RACE IN OUR CITY. IN OUR COUNTRY, TOO.

MARCH 1, 2020:
SOUTH BEND, INDIANA

ABOUT A YEAR-AND-HALF AGO, MY HUSBAND CAME FROM WORK TO TELL ME –

WELL, HE ASKED ME –

WE HAVE A RESPONSIBILITY TO CONSIDER THE EFFECT OF REMAINING IN THIS RACE ANY FURTHER. WE MUST RECOGNIZE THEN AT THIS POINT IN THE RACE, THE BEST WAY TO KEEP FAITH WITH OUR GOALS AND IDEALS IS TO STEP ASIDE AND HELP BRING OUR PARTY AND OUR COUNTRY TOGETHER.

"WHAT DO YOU THINK ABOUT RUNNING FOR PRESIDENT?"

AND I LAUGHED. NOT AT HIM, BUT AT LIFE.

YOUR VOTE 2020

IN A FIELD IN WHICH MORE THAN TWO DOZEN DEMOCRATIC CANDIDATES RAN FOR PRESIDENT — SENATORS AND GOVERNORS, BILLIONAIRES, A FORMER VICE PRESIDENT — WE ACHIEVED A TOP FOUR FINISH IN EACH OF THE FIRST FOUR STATES.

YOUR VOTE 2020 abc NEWS

WE FOUND COUNTLESS AMERICANS READY TO SUPPORT A MIDDLE-CLASS MILLENNIAL MAYOR FROM THE INDUSTRIAL MIDWEST, NOT IN SPITE OF THAT EXPERIENCE BUT BECAUSE OF IT, EAGER TO GET WASHINGTON TO START WORKING LIKE OUR BEST-RUN COMMUNITIES.

I MADE THE DIFFICULT DECISION TO SUSPEND MY CAMPAIGN FOR THE PRESIDENCY. I WILL DO EVERYTHING IN MY POWER TO ENSURE THAT WE HAVE A NEW DEMOCRATIC PRESIDENT COME JANUARY.

YOU HAVEN'T HEARD THE LAST FROM ME. I'M JUST GETTING STARTED.

TIDALWAVE
COMICS

Michael Frizell — Writer

Juan José Pereyra — Art

Darren G. Davis — Editor

Benjamin Glibert — Letters

Dave Ryan — Cover

Darren G. Davis
Publisher

Maggie Jessup
Publicity

Susan Ferris
Entertainment Manager

TIDALWAVE
PRODUCTIONS

TIDALWAVE

LEGENDS ARE BORN. **TIDALWAVE** PRODUCTIONS

CPSIA information can be obtained
at www.ICGtesting.com
Printed in the USA
LVHW021053211220
674729LV00007B/285